Help Your Child Cope with
Change

HELP YOUR CHILD COPE WITH CHANGE

An Hachette UK Company
www.hachette.co.uk

Vie Books, an imprint of Summersdale Publishers Ltd
Part of Octopus Publishing Group Limited
Carmelite House
50 Victoria Embankment
LONDON
EC4Y 0DZ
UK

www.summersdale.com

Printed and bound in China

ISBN: 978-1-80007-194-0

Substantial discounts on bulk quantities of Summersdale books are available to corporations, professional associations and other organizations. For details contact general enquiries: telephone: +44 (0) 1243 771107 or email: enquiries@summersdale.com.

Disclaimer
Every effort has been made to ensure that the information in this book is accurate and current at the time of publication. The author and the publisher cannot accept responsibility for any misuse or misunderstanding of any information contained herein, or any loss, damage or injury, be it health, financial or otherwise, suffered by any individual or group acting upon or relying on information contained herein. None of the opinions or suggestions in this book are intended to replace medical opinion. If you have concerns about your health or that of a child in your care, please seek professional advice.

Permission has been sought for the Kübler-Ross Grief Cycle diagram on p.22

Help Your Child Cope with
Change

What to Know, Say and Do
When Times Are Tough

Liat Hughes Joshi

Contents

Introduction

Experiencing change is an inescapable part of being human. A life where nothing altered for better or worse would quickly become boring. Change, however, is not always comfortable – it can be scary, bewildering, and sometimes exciting, or all of these things at the same time.

This is often more intense for children, who might not fully understand what's happening or the implications. On top of this, change tends to occur "to" children – major life events are usually either due to parents' or others' decisions (to separate or move house, for example), or they're seemingly random and beyond anyone's control (such as a bereavement or the impact of a pandemic).

When your child is hit by change, whatever the cause, it'll make a world of difference to know you're by their side – in the boat with them to navigate choppy seas together – with practical support, advice, well-being ideas and, of course, love and a hug.

That's what this book is all about – making it easier for you to do that in realistic ways. Think of it as your family's toolkit to see you through tough times.

About this book

Whether your child is in the middle of dealing with a major life event right now or you've bought this book to build their resilience so they can cope with future issues, its tips and advice are here to help you to help them.

You can read the book from cover to cover or dip in and choose the sections most relevant or helpful for your child, depending on the situation they're facing and what will appeal or work for them as an individual. Of course, no single tip will magic away all hurt, worry and upset. But take a few together, and they can make a meaningful difference.

You'll find chapters about how children (and adults) react to change, strategies for coping with specific life events such as bereavement, parental divorce, moving home or school, and ideas for general well-being boosters, plus advice on seeking further professional help.

You matter too

The book has been written with five- to 16-year-olds in mind but there's also a section to help you cope with change better, because how a parent manages difficulties influences their child's feelings in turn. Plus, if you're not dealing well with a big life event, that makes it more challenging to assist your child.

CHAPTER 1

Understanding children and change

If we want to help our children cope with life events, it's useful to get to know a bit more about the context of how we humans tend to react to change. With this in mind, the following pages cover a couple of theories and general ideas about this.

You'll know from your own life that people's responses even to very similar changes can vary, yet there are some behaviours and emotions that are pretty universal. Understanding these can provide a useful backdrop when supporting your child, although don't be too concerned if their reality doesn't follow the theory or models.

Evolution has shaped the way we react to change

Over hundreds of thousands of years, we humans have evolved to react to danger in ways that are meant to help us survive. This all shapes how we respond to some of the changes we face, even though we're now more likely to hunt for our dinner in a supermarket aisle than, say, on a savannah while trying to dodge a pack of lions who want to make us their meal instead. Put very simply, faced with a threat (or a perceived threat), there are two phases to what happens to us.*

First, there's our initial, instinctive and emotional response when it's "all systems go", where there's the equivalent of a siren blaring and red warning lights flashing in our brains and bodies. Our heart rate and breathing quickens, and the hormones adrenalin and cortisol come flooding in. Even our blood flow changes – away from our heart and more toward our limbs to help us run or punch. It is all about making it easier to react quickly to whatever is going on, be it a bear prowling around our prehistoric cave or a noise at night in our cosy modern home (when we wonder if it's a burglar).

This is the mode when we might be upset, scared or angry, when we have those big and powerful feelings. It's sometimes called "fight or flight" because we're geared up to fight or run!

After this, at some stage, we can settle down and think more clearly and switch to the part of our brains that deals with things in a relatively calm and rational way. That's when we can work out how we really feel about a change – our ancestors might have pondered what they could do to make things safer when they went out hunting if they saw those hungry lions again.

Understanding this is super-helpful as you – and, in time, your child – can then recognize that how you feel in the "Argh! Danger!" phase is only temporary and that you can calm yourself down and reach the second phase a little quicker.

* If you want to learn more about this, check out Daniel Kahneman's book, *Thinking, Fast and Slow*.

... and given us an inbuilt negativity bias

Let's stay in prehistoric times for another page... Imagine this, you're out in that savannah of an evening. Would it be a wise idea to be so captivated by the beauty of the sunset that you miss the threat of the lions creeping up behind you? Probably not. And it's this sort of situation that seems to have led us to evolve what's called "negativity bias".

This means that when we're making judgements and assessing situations, we often focus more on negatives than positives. It also applies to the impressions we build of other people – for instance, in studies where participants have been given descriptions of someone's good and bad traits, the participants processed and used the negative information more than the positive, even when the researchers tried to match the intensity of both sets of descriptions.

Again, help with this is on its way if you read on, as we're going to look at ways of adding a dash more positivity to rebalance in the face of negativity bias.

A moment of reflection

It might be worth thinking back over how you've dealt with big changes in your own life – as a child and more recently – to recall how you felt and what helped you process these challenging times. Take two or three events from your past and reflect on:

- How did you react to each one initially?

- How did your feelings evolve over time?

- What differed with your reaction and what was the same with each of the events and why? Particularly focus on any events from your childhood here.

- What helped you? What can you learn from these experiences?

Ways children experience change differently to adults

No matter how grown-up our kids can sometimes appear, they really do deal with change differently to us – for better or worse.

Here are some of the reasons why they might not perceive and respond to the same change situation in the way grown-ups around them do:

- As adults, we can draw on our past experiences. Even if we have not seen the exact situation that is happening right now before, we know that things do usually improve – pain tends to fade, emotions settle down, shock lessens. Children don't have much of a back catalogue of prior experience to reassure them.

- Grown-ups tend to have more control – okay, not all the time, but we're more likely to be able to shape events or at least practical matters in response to whatever is happening. Not being able to have control can leave children feeling more vulnerable and fearful, although conversely being responsible can of course sometimes be stressful for parents.

- We don't have so much "magical thinking", which can lead children to feel they are to blame for things that they didn't actually cause. For example, believing that if they had behaved better the last time they saw their grandparent, then Grandma or Grandpa wouldn't have become ill; or believing that their parent wouldn't have lost their job had they not been so loud during Mum or Dad's conference calls.

- Younger children are less likely to be able to understand their feelings and emotions than adults – they might not even know the vocabulary to describe them to themselves or others. This can be confusing or even scary.

The "Change Curve"

The "Change Curve" is a well-known way of explaining reactions to change, developed in the late 1960s by Elisabeth Kübler-Ross, a Swiss-American psychiatrist. It's also sometimes called the Kübler-Ross model, or the "five stages of grief".

Over five decades on, it's still used widely and is applicable to all sorts of more significant change and loss situations, including bereavement, separation and serious illness. Someone's response to smaller changes might also involve these stages to some degree. The model is not specifically about children but is relevant to all age groups.

Here's a description of the stages – although note that your child may not follow these exactly or in the order below. They might skip a stage or overlap between them, showing signs of more than one stage on the same day or switching back and forth. We still think it's a useful way of considering their reactions and helping to understand them.

1. Denial

Usually the first reaction. Here your child might avoid the reality of what's happening, feel confused, shocked, numb, overwhelmed and / or afraid. Interestingly, this phase might be our mind's way of coping with difficult news – it allows us to pace our feelings.

> What your child might do or say: distract themselves, throw themselves into an activity and act like nothing has happened.
>
> "It's not true", "I don't care!", "You're making it up!"

2. Anger

The situation starts to feel more real and unavoidable – it's hitting home and it's harder to pretend and just carry on. Now your child might feel a mix of frustrated, irritated, furious and anxious.

> What your child might do or say: blame or redirect their anger at someone or something (often a parent or sibling), even if that person or thing isn't the actual cause. They might also show visible anger and aggression now.
>
> "This is not fair", "Why has this happened to me/us?"

3. Bargaining

Your child is still struggling to accept the reality of the situation and is hoping something can change it back to before. They might also be reaching out to others for help or advice, or telling their story of what has happened or is happening.

What your child might do or say: younger children might engage in magical thinking – trying to bargain away the situation – for example, asking if Grandpa can come back to life or you won't get divorced if they promise to be well-behaved forever. They might make wishes or pray (if they are religious) now too.

"I will never complain about anything if you and Mum/Dad can get back together", "If I close my eyes and think lots of good thoughts, will he stop being so ill?"

4. Depression

This next stage can be especially challenging for parents to witness – your child might be overwhelmed by sadness and helplessness. Note that showing the signs of depression (see page 34) in the aftermath of a significant change doesn't mean your child has clinical depression. Providing support and encouraging them to get professional help if needed can make a big difference.

What your child might do or say: they might become withdrawn, or cry a lot.

"I don't want to do anything or go anywhere", "I can't stop crying."

5. Acceptance

Your child is now accepting what has happened and the new situations it has brought. That doesn't mean they are necessarily happy about it all though.

What your child might do or say: they are no longer fighting the situation or showing anger about it. Where they have influence over what happens in their life, they can make more reasonable choices and have discussions about options.

"I'm okay", "I miss Grandma but I'm glad she isn't suffering any more."

DEPRESSION AND DETACHMENT

Overwhelmed
Lack of energy
Helplessness
Hostility

DENIAL

Avoidance
Confusion
Fear
Numbness
Blame

ANGER

Frustration
Anxiety
Irritation
Shame

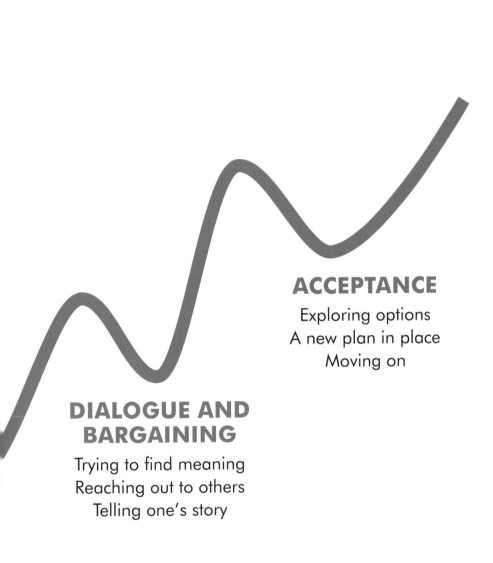

ACCEPTANCE
Exploring options
A new plan in place
Moving on

DIALOGUE AND BARGAINING
Trying to find meaning
Reaching out to others
Telling one's story

CHAPTER 2

Laying the foundations for future resilience

Resilience is the ability to deal with, and recover from, problems, and it's crucial for our mental health and happiness. It can have a significant impact beyond the obvious one of bouncing back from life's inevitable knocks too, since resilient people also tend to be more confident and less fearful of failure. This is because they know that they can pick themselves up again if things do go wrong. So, it's certainly something very much worth encouraging in your child. Some people and personality types do seem to have a predisposition to being more or less resilient, but there are definitely ways of thinking and approaching situations that will help your child build this characteristic over time.

Show emotions not a "stiff upper lip"

Resilience absolutely doesn't mean supressing feelings – it's not about a "stiff upper lip" and denying natural, human responses to adversity. Rather, it's about "allowing" our feelings, being aware of them and then handling them constructively when we're ready to do so – ourselves or with the help of others.

If your child seems to be holding strong feelings in, you can call upon some of the ideas in Chapter 3 to try and encourage them to express these, and reassure them that these feelings are normal.

It's also important to be a good role model here; it can be tempting to put a brave face on in front of your child but that doesn't mean you have to pretend you aren't upset or struggling at times too. You don't need to hide all your own feelings. Quite the reverse: you'll do your child more favours by demonstrating how you manage them, the healthy ways you help yourself feel better and how you get support.

Be your child's coach and adviser, not their fixer

It's tempting to try to smooth over every issue your child faces but, no matter how well-meaning this might be, if you always jump in, they'll be less likely to build problem-solving skills and confidence. Think of it like this: if you're constantly hovering, ready with a lifebuoy to rescue them, your child won't need to learn to swim.

When you can, instead of being their fixer, try to be more of a coach and source of wisdom, nurturing their ability to tackle challenges themselves but with your support. Ask questions to encourage this: "How do you think the other person was feeling?", "What could you do to make this better?", "If you were advising a friend in this situation, what would you suggest?"

This can start small – perhaps letting a younger child resolve a squabble over whose turn it is to have a toy – and move on to bigger problems in time. Here's an example: if there's an issue at school, depending on your child's age and the severity, instead of you going in or emailing about it, encourage your child to talk with their teacher, planning and practising what they might say about it in advance together if needed.

If they don't get this right first time, that's okay – again, don't criticize but help them learn what they could do better, so that they're not afraid to try and fail.

Foster realistic positivity and optimism

Being at least reasonably positive around your child will rub off on them – it's tough sometimes but try to model optimism and sensitively highlight upsides of a situation where appropriate.

Even in the darkest of times there can be some brightness and hope; it's just that we might need to look harder for it and switch off those negative thoughts. Clearly, this doesn't mean trying to look on the bright side in the midst of a tragic or traumatic event, but it can involve gently introducing an optimistic element, when the time is right.

So perhaps after the death of a grandparent, acknowledge how much you'll all miss them and how sad you are, but also that you've been incredibly fortunate to have had such a wonderful Grandpa or Grandma in your lives – and you'll have memories of them that you can cherish forever.

A comment like this will never make someone's grief magically disappear but it can introduce a ray of light – a more positive approach – to adversity.

Encourage "thinking time"

Look back to when you were a child and chances are you had a lot more unscheduled time than your own children do. Perhaps it was boring sometimes but you had much more space to ponder what was going on in your life.

Now digital devices mean there's something to occupy us wherever we are, with a mere click or swipe of a screen, and modern children often have far fuller calendars of after-school classes, activities, outings and play dates.

But having "free thinking time" to daydream and reflect is hugely valuable to process what's going on in our lives.

It's hard to suddenly introduce this without moans of "I'm bored!" but, ideally, get your child used to spending time with their own thoughts, rather than allowing them a device constantly so they're always doing something and being entertained.

Distinguish between mental health conditions and everyday emotions

We often hear people casually say that they're anxious or depressed when they mean they're feeling worried, stressed or unhappy, but true anxiety and depression are clinical conditions and distinct from these regular, everyday emotions. They're more persistent and more significant in their impact – they start to get in the way of your child participating in normal life and their usual activities.

It's healthy for children to begin to learn the distinction between everyday feelings and mental health conditions for themselves, so they'll know when they might need to get outside support. Talking about the difference in a natural way in casual conversations will help build an understanding of this.

If your child is showing signs of being anxious or depressed (see the following pages), we recommend you seek further support – see Chapter 8. The techniques throughout the book might still be useful but they're not a substitute for professional help for mental health conditions.

Here are some scenarios to provide a feel for the difference between mental health conditions and everyday emotions:

Examples of feeling sad or worried	Examples of depression or anxiety
Being stressed the night before a test or exam or having a few spells of feeling agitated about revision.	Not being able to sleep or eat for several weeks before exams, obsessively cramming revision into every waking moment and refusing to take a break.
Crying after falling out with a friend.	Having a very low mood and refusing to see friends or do things they previously enjoyed for a period of weeks.
Being upset by a close relative's death and having tearful spells from time to time but also being able to return to a relatively normal daily life, at least gradually.	Withdrawing from wanting to spend time with people and doing activities that they previously normally like for a sustained period – typically more than a week or two.

Signs of depression...

"Depression is a common and serious medical illness that negatively affects how you feel, the way you think and how you act. [It] causes feelings of sadness and/or a loss of interest in activities you once enjoyed. It can lead to a variety of emotional and physical problems and decrease your ability to function at work* and at home."

– The American Psychiatric Association (APA) (www.psychiatry.org). The APA adds that symptoms must last at least two weeks.

In the midst or aftermath of serious and difficult changes, from bereavement to parents separating, it is of course possible that a child might develop clinical depression, so it's sensible to be aware of the physical and/or emotional effects to look out for. Note that not all of the signs below need to be present to suggest your child might have depression.

* For children, "at work" can be replaced with "at school".

Typical signs of depression:

- Irritability, tearfulness and anger

- A persistent sadness that you can't encourage your child out of – for example, to do things they usually want to do

- Lethargy and unresponsiveness – like they no longer care

- Trouble sleeping or sleeping more than normal

- Losing interest in things they used to enjoy such as seeing friends or relatives or going out to do something fun

- Self-harming, or considering self-harming

- Eating less than normal, or overeating

- Difficulty concentrating

- Feeling worthless

- Having suicidal thoughts

If your child is depressed or suicidal, seek immediate support from your doctor or mental health service or ring a helpline (see Chapter 8).

Signs of anxiety

A degree of stress and worry is to be expected when we're facing big changes and challenges and this can be a positive coping mechanism, galvanizing us into action. But sometimes these "normal" human emotions can get out of hand.

According to the APA, to be diagnosed with an anxiety disorder, the fear or anxiety must "be out of proportion to the situation or age inappropriate" and "hinder [the person's] ability to function normally". If you think this could be happening to your child, here's what to look out for.

Typical signs of anxiety:

- Irritability, tearfulness and anger
- Episodes of feeling panicked, which can include difficulty breathing
- Struggling to sleep or eat properly
- Stomach upsets or aches
- Bed-wetting
- Problems concentrating
- Losing interest in things they used to enjoy such as seeing friends or relatives or going out to do something fun
- Overwhelmingly negative thinking
- Becoming withdrawn
- Physical ticks

As their parent, you know your child best and what their "normal" is. Is how they are behaving unusual *for them*? Are there any patterns that have changed? Is their behaviour different all the time or just in certain situations / in response to particular triggers?

CHAPTER 3

Effective talking and listening

Talking with trust and openness is vital for strong parent-child relationships at the best of times, but even more so at the worst of times. Just as a doctor needs to be able to diagnose an illness before they can treat it, you have to know what your child is thinking and feeling to help them cope with the situation they're in. Talking and listening to your child is not just essential for this; it encourages them to develop emotional intelligence and awareness too. This chapter suggests ideas to promote open communication about these issues.

Listen up!

As parents we want to smooth things over for our kids as soon as possible when they're struggling, making it tempting to dive in with solutions and advice, but it's vital to listen to what they really think and feel first.

Being a good listener means giving your undivided attention, not interrupting, showing you're fully tuned in with body language and verbal cues (those "mmm"s and "okay"s), and now and then reflecting back what your child is saying ("So I'm hearing that you're worried about making friends when you move school").

Your child will appreciate being truly listened to and it'll mean you're responding to their real feelings, not your perceptions of them.

Even if you're a good listener, your child may still find discussing difficult situations a challenge: they might not understand their feelings enough to be able to describe them, or they might be too overcome with anger or fear to talk calmly. They might also be afraid they'll worry, upset or annoy you, or might be worried that you'll tease or embarrass them.

Pick your talking time and place

Choose somewhere you'll both be relaxed and without distractions – at a café with a treat (as long as this is private enough so your child won't feel overheard), during a walk in the park, or cuddled up on the sofa.

With pre-teens and teens, a chat side by side in the car while you're driving can work wonders to get them to open up with less awkwardness as they can avoid eye contact.

If these options might be too intense, you could try doing an activity you both enjoy but which still allows conversation. Anything from bowling to baking to a bike ride – whatever you find appealing.

When it comes to timing, if possible, avoid sharing difficult news or starting heavy conversations when your child might be hungry or tired, such as at the end of a long school day or just before bedtime.

Provide prompts

Prompts can "oil" conversations, helping children to open up, especially if they're feeling shy or awkward or you or they simply don't know where to begin.

Here are some ideas for conversation starters:

- Tell a (truthful) story from your own childhood about a similar experience which you can then relate to their current situation.

- Watch a film or TV programme, or read a storybook or novel together involving similar themes – although you might want to check beforehand how the scenario is portrayed (those which feature significant trauma or unhappy endings might not set the right tone).

- A self-help guide such as *No More Worries!* by Poppy O'Neill (Vie, 2021) can be great for older children to work through, then talk about together.

- Model being open by discussing your own emotions about the situation (if it affects you too) and then asking if they feel the same or differently.

- Ask broader questions about how they're feeling, how their day was or what they're happy or unhappy about right now, then drill down to specifics of what's going on in their life.

Find out their real, actual feelings

Every child and situation is different and you need to find out how *your* child really, actually feels right now rather than making assumptions about this. Not the narrative from the media or the movies, not how you or their sibling feels, but them as the wonderfully unique individual they are.

It's worth noting that children can be quite resilient and don't always react as badly to change as we think. For example, there's a general idea out there that all children are distraught when their parents break the news that they're separating – but sometimes this can be a relief to them if there has been a lot of conflict in the family home.

Help them to name their emotions

With younger children especially, you might need to help them learn descriptions of what they are feeling, be it anger, frustration, excitement or something else. Gently doing this for them ("I can see that you feel angry / upset") can help your child understand their emotions, plus they'll know that they are being heard and understood by you. But do ensure that, as per the previous page, you're not making an incorrect assumption about how they feel and foisting it on them.

As a bonus, whatever our age, research has shown that labelling our feelings can make them less intense, reducing the response in the fight-or-flight part of the brain so we can switch into our thinking-more-calmly mode.

Don't dismiss your child's reality, tease or mock them

"Don't be silly!", "Why on earth would you think that?", "You *should* be happy about the new baby / house / step-parent!"… Rare is the child who has heard these types of comments and thought, "You're right, I *am* being silly so I will be delighted about this," and changed their feelings. The fact is that telling your child how they *should* react doesn't change how they *actually* feel, and can make it seem like their parent isn't listening to them or respecting their emotions, which can exacerbate rather than ease their stress or confusion.

Even if what your child is saying seems irrational to your grown-up mind, it is their reality, so it's important to address that rather than brush it aside or undermine their honest feelings.

It's especially inadvisable to tease or mock children when they have confided in you – if you do this, in future they might fear embarrassment and not share things again.

Use open-ended questions for open conversations

Questions that can be answered with a "yes", "no" or "okay" aren't going to get communication going between you as well as open-ended ones, especially if your child is shy, feeling awkward or having a rather monosyllabic phase as a teenager.

Compare the closed questions below with the open alternatives – can you see how the second options might give your child space to explore their answer?

Instead of this... (closed question)	Ask this... (open question)
Are you sad?	How do you feel about X?
Are you worried?	Can you try to explain what you're worrying about?

Draft in "agony aunts" (or uncles, grandparents or family friends)

It's not a reflection on the strength of your relationship with your child if, for whatever reason, they're not willing or able to discuss their feelings about changes in their life with you. As an alternative, is there someone else they trust who they might feel comfortable talking to – an aunt, uncle, grandparent or family friend perhaps? If you do go down this route, their confidante will need to be upfront about whether they're going to share what they're told with you, otherwise your child might feel their confidence has been betrayed.

CHAPTER 4

Supporting your child through tough times

This chapter provides tips and advice to help steer your child through when they're in the midst of dealing with a problematic change. Realistically, no single tactic will individually and instantly make everything okay, but a few of these ideas taken together can make quite a difference.

There are more suggestions specific to bereavement, parental divorce, moving house, having a new sibling and changing school in Chapter 6.

Retain routines

When aspects of your child's life are unpredictable, confusing or even frightening, the more of their usual routine you can keep to, the better. This can be quite a challenge if there's lots of change going on in your family, but if possible, sticking to their usual mealtimes, bedtimes, clubs and activities will be reassuring and grounding, creating a sense of security.

Consistent times to sleep and eat will also ensure that your child is well-rested, and reduce the chances of "hangriness" – as some people like to call hunger-induced grouchiness.

If life is in flux for your family more generally – such as after a separation – it'll be beneficial to create new routines and traditions, such as those for birthdays or the festive season, to replace any that have been lost.

Record your child's moods

Keeping a diary of how your child is feeling and what's going on in their life during a period of change will make it easier to spot any patterns to their behaviour and how specific triggers affect them (positively or negatively). After a few days, you might well start to see trends which can suggest potential solutions. If they write the diary themselves, it will also help your child to understand what influences their emotions and moods.

Some parents find it more convenient to create an informal digital diary in the notes section of their phone, so that it's pretty much always to hand. If you or your child favour paper, another option is to draw out a chart with columns for meals, sleep times and the day's activities plus their mood alongside them. Younger children could draw their emotions with a smiley face or use different colours to describe them.

The diary will also prove useful if you need to seek professional support, helping you and your child to share a record of what's been going on in their life and their reactions to it.

Give a little leeway (but not too much)

It's natural and normal to feel angry, upset or stressed sometimes, but it's important for your child to understand that they should not express that in ways which damage things or hurt other people, especially those who love and are trying to care for them.

If your child does or says something that would usually be unacceptable – for instance, they hit you or a sibling, or break a toy or gadget in anger – you might want to be a shade gentler than normal in your approach, taking into account the severity of the situation they currently face. But do still let them know that this behaviour is wrong and there will be consequences if it continues. Keep the period when they get any extra leeway as short as possible before re-establishing your usual rules and expectations – strong boundaries will actually make your child feel secure.

Change the channel

We all have times when the thoughts running through our heads – our inner voice – are negative, when we focus on our worst-case scenarios and fears. Help your child to understand that just in the same way they can change a song or a TV channel, they can also switch to different music or programmes for their thinking – retuning to more positive, happier thoughts.

Younger children could actually pretend they're pressing a button on their head or their hand, or grab the real TV remote and imagine it's switching over their thinking to the happier channel.

Swap specs

Remember the classic phrase "looking through rose-tinted glasses", expressing how we sometimes don a warm filter, viewing something more positively than it warrants? We can also do this in the opposite direction – as though we have put on grey-tinted glasses – filtering things through a negative, gloomier, down-in-the-dumps lens.

Clearly, more serious situations such as a bereavement do not lend themselves to putting on rose-tinted specs but others, perhaps moving house or school, are more subjective in their impact and more likely to have pros and cons.

Can your child swap between imaginary pairs of glasses with different coloured lenses to "view" the upsides and downsides of the situation they're in? You could even make some pairs of specs with pink, grey or whatever colours they like, with tissue paper or cellophane.

What do they "see" differently when wearing their positive pink lenses compared to the gloomy grey ones? If they feel better with the pink specs, could they pretend to keep them on to see things more optimistically for the rest of the day?

Share mantras

When we're overwhelmed with emotion and struggling to stay calm, it's useful to have a few set lines we can recall easily to draw strength and focus from. Teach these to your children so they can grab hold of them to drown out any negative or scary thoughts — you might need to change the wording for younger ones.

This too shall pass / The sun will shine again

When we're faced with difficulties, invariably things do get better; life won't always feel this wretched and time really does heal. For younger children, "the sun will shine again" is a simple, reassuring concept to grasp.

One step at a time / Bird by bird

There's a well-known anecdote from author Anne Lamott. Her brother was feeling overwhelmed by a school project about birds which he'd left to the last minute. Anne's father reassured his son that all he had to do was take things bird by bird. The moral of the story is that when a problem feels too big to cope with, we can make it a lot easier by approaching it one step at a time.

Stick with the good people

If something has happened in your child's life which has been caused by ill-intentioned individuals, help them focus on the idea that most people are good and decent. There's almost always someone good in their lives. Stick with the lovely people.

Bash away bad thoughts

Symbolically getting rid of negative or frightening thoughts can be surprisingly cathartic – even if the effects are temporary, it can lift your child's mood. Here are some ideas on how you can do this:

Bursting bubbles

This one's a stress reliever and positivity exercise for younger children. Grab some bubble mix and together blow a load of bubbles. Before or during each set of bubbles being blown, have your child name the emotions they want to be rid of and then encourage them to burst those bubbles to help that negative feeling go away too.

Gobble concerns up with a worry eater

Is there a kindly, brave teddy or toy that could symbolically gobble up your child's concerns? Have them write or draw the upsetting thoughts or feelings before "feeding them" to the helpful toy! Similarly, you could create and decorate a worry box, with a slot your little one can post away their worries into.

Floating off feelings

Having a flower, twig or leaf represent an emotion and letting it float away into the sea or river can be really symbolic. Your child could tie a (biodegradable) paper tag on to a flower stem, writing their worry on the tag.

Distinguish between "can change" and "can't change" issues

Many times in life, we are faced with situations we can do nothing about, but that doesn't make us entirely helpless; we are still able to change our responses – what we think, feel and do.

Children, however, can get quite confused about what they can alter and what they have no control over. You can alleviate this by talking through the areas they can and can't shape.

Sit down together with a blank piece of paper and write or draw the things that are set in stone in a particular scenario and those that they do have some say about, under two columns – "can change" and "can't change".

Here's an example: if you and their other parent are separating, your child might believe that they can somehow stop this happening. This thinking can prevent them from accepting and processing reality, so you'll need to clarify that this is not the case and no matter what they say or do, it will not change the outcome. However, then look at aspects of the situation they *can* alter. Are they old enough to have some say on when they will be with each parent? What can they determine about how they react – for example, how they tell their friends about the separation? Can they choose which toys go to which house or the decoration of their new bedroom?

Can change

Can't change

Find the positives

As mentioned earlier (see page 14), we humans do have a tendency to focus more on the bad aspects of a situation, rather than positives, with our inbuilt negativity bias.

To help rebalance this thinking, write a list with your child of a few upsides to counter the downsides of the situation.

So, if your family is moving house, your child might complain about the garden being smaller, which is not so good to play in, and how they don't like their bedroom decoration. However, you could rebalance this by mentioning some positives. Perhaps there's a playroom or they'll have a larger bedroom, a shorter journey to school or you'll be closer to their best friend's home.

Obviously, there's a time and a place for this approach. It will only be worthwhile if there are some genuine positives to the situation that are not too distant in the future and that your child is ready to hear and will value.

For instance, if they're upset about the prospect of the arrival of a much younger sibling, step- or half-sibling, there's little point suggesting that it will be lovely to have a sister or brother around when they're both adults and the age gap seems less important. When you're a kid, you're more focused on the here and now and the near future.

Encourage basic anger management

Anger is a completely normal human emotion but the key is to channel that anger safely and appropriately, rather than, for example, hitting or screaming at loved ones.

The challenge is that when we are angry and we're flooded with emotions, it's not so easy to think clearly and behave well; we can lose control. Sometimes, we have to try and trick ourselves into calming down so we can think more clearly. To help make this happen, get your child to choose a single word or very short phrase that they can learn to "grab" when they feel themselves getting angry (or even better, when they experience something they have learned triggers their anger), which then reminds them to do their calm-down action.

Once your child is calmer, encourage them to reflect on what made them angry to help them understand their triggers and responses.

Ideas include:

Calm word	Calm-down action
"Breathe"	Breathe deeply for a count of ten
"Count"	Count forward or backward for ten
"Colour" – or the name of their favourite colour	Close their eyes and visualize the colour
"Relax"	Shrug shoulders, breathe and relax their shoulders a few times to ease tension
A pet's name	Imagine stroking the pet if it is not there and they can't actually do so

Break down their worries

When we feel overwhelmed with worry or fear, it can be quite a challenge to see the wood for the trees – to spot what the solutions are to our problems and keep perspective. It all just feels like TOO MUCH! By breaking down our worries into smaller chunks, we can start to identify actions we might take to improve a situation or reflect that, actually, things are not so bad and we can cope after all.

Grab some paper and have your child write down – or draw – each worry or task and then beside it add an action or realistic solution to it. If they struggle to explain what exactly they are worried or afraid of, perhaps saying "everything", suggest they give you their top three worries.

If you want to take this a step further, you could also get them to score each item on their list out of ten for its importance and then score how easy the solution is to sort out – this will help them prioritize which issues to tackle first. Anything that is both a big, high-scoring worry and rates highly for being quick and easy to solve should go on top of their to-do list.

Here's an example: your child is worried about moving house.

Worry	Action
I won't be able to sleep.	Keep to your usual bedtime routine, bedding, etc.
It just won't be as nice.	Identify three favourite things that make your existing home appealing that will be coming with you, or similar substitutes at the new house.
I'll be too far from my friends.	Discuss how you can still meet up and arrange an initial social event.
Your bedroom is too far from mine.	Buy or borrow a walkie-talkie or intercom for the first few nights.

Ring-fence some daily quality time

During difficult periods, ensure you and your child have as much time as possible together when you can talk or hug or just hang out without distractions such as mobile phones or household tasks. Try to prioritize some one-to-one time every day. Even 10 minutes at bedtime will allow them to share worries, get reassurance or simply feel heard and less alone.

Classic, simple family activities such as board games, a walk in the park, a bike ride, watching a TV series together cuddled up on the sofa, or a café trip for a milkshake... it's all good stuff and encourages strong relationships more generally too.

Assemble a well-being first-aid kit

Put together a well-being first-aid box or bag to keep at hand, perhaps in their bedroom, for when your child feels worried, sad or overwhelmed. They could choose a few items that have a positive, relaxing effect on them, such as:

- Something tactile that they can stroke or squish – a piece of fabric, a velvety teddy bear, a smooth pebble

- Favourite song lyrics or poems written out, or a special letter or card

- A photo of a favourite memory, place or people

- A treasured possession

- Something with a calming scent, such as a soap or room spray

- An object that is mesmerizing to look at – for example, a snow globe or lava lamp

- Bubble wrap or plasticine to play with

- A note to themselves with some of the other ideas in this book such as their well-being boost menu (see page 73), a letter of encouragement or an inspiring quote or motto

CHAPTER 5

Well-being boosts

While our previous chapter covered ways to help your child process and cope more directly with adversity and its impact, this next one provides ideas for some general well-being boosts – little sources of joy or calm to call upon when your child needs a lift. They're also things that over time your son or daughter might start to recognize as self-care tactics to deploy themselves when they're feeling low or stressed.

Not all of them will appeal to all children or suit their temperament but there are plenty of options here, so hopefully there's something for everyone.

Meditate

Meditation is a well-being go-to for many people nowadays and for good reason – it's free, you can do it pretty much anytime and anywhere, and it's effective. It's not just about relaxation at stressful times – meditation has a raft of benefits for children (and adults too) including improved concentration, focus and sleep.

Children's meditation doesn't need to be serious or daunting and nor does it have to involve "om"s and Buddhas if that's not for you. There are loads of free guided meditations with appeal for all ages online, but equally it can be as simple as just clearing your mind and refocusing thoughts. There are ideas on how to do this on the next page.

Before you start, your child needs to be somewhere quiet and comfortable, and should ideally be lying down with their eyes closed.

Here are some child-friendly meditations to try – even a minute or two of these can work wonders:

Super-simple meditation

You definitely don't have to be experienced meditation gurus for this one. Have your child place their hand on their tummy and focus on their breath as they breathe in and out. Can they feel their stomach rise and fall? Can they slow down their breathing and count for three or four as they breathe in and three or four as they breathe out?

Brilliant belly balloon breaths

Have your child imagine there's a balloon in their belly – as they breathe in, they should visualize it inflating… bigger and bigger… and as they breathe out, it deflates… down and down… smaller and smaller…

Body journey

Take your child on a journey from toe to top. First ask them to inhale slowly and exhale a few times to slow their breathing. Then, starting with their toes, tense and relax them, squeezing out all that tension, then their whole foot, then calf muscles, thigh muscles... you get the picture... right to the top, ending with their lips, their tongue, their eyes. Finish off with some more slow, deep breaths.

Square breathing

Breathe in to a count of four, hold to a count of four, breathe out to a count of four and then hold... you guessed it... to a count of four. Repeat three or four times. As your child breathes "along" each side of the square (with one side of the square per inhale, one per exhale, etc.), they could trace their finger along the edges of a small box or draw a square with their finger on a table or desk (if they are sitting up somewhere) or in the air.

Noticing nature

Studies show that being around nature can make a significant difference to our well-being. The outdoors is quite literally right on all our doorsteps; even the most urban location has trees or a park nearby.

If it's a cloudy, breezy day, sit down on a bench or lie on a patch of grass and quietly watch the clouds sailing past, solely focusing on them. If it's raining, observe raindrops dancing onto a puddle or ripples on the water's surface caused by the wind. Watch the sun slowly going down or listen to the birdsong – close your eyes and really, really listen. All this is about focusing on one thing at a time and one thing alone, clearing your mind of all else and learning to appreciate the beauty of the natural world.

Activate some activity

It's widely recognized that exercise releases feel-good endorphins, is healthy for our bodies and can make us more likely to sleep better too. You can do it alone, in a team, make it long or short, and be outside of the home, near home or at home – it's all good!

Ideas: a walk in the park or woods (combining exercise with a nature fix!), a jog round the block, a bike ride, a short exercise video, jumping jacks, skipping or a kitchen disco dancing session.

Sports which involve hitting something – tennis, squash or even boxing – can also be especially good stress-relieving exercise for all ages as a controlled and constructive outlet for letting off steam.

Create a "happy menu"

Ask your child what makes them feel good. Put together a menu of coping mechanisms and distractions they can draw upon when they need a boost. If they're stuck, discuss what works for you and make suggestions – this can be really small and even quite silly things: life's little joys.

A "happy menu" could look something like this:

- Watching some comedy or sharing jokes ("laughter is the best medicine", as the phrase goes)

- Hugging

- Listening to music – something fun and lively

- Dancing (even just around the living room)

- Helping other people / volunteering

- Spending time with a pet

- Doing arts and crafts

Look after the basics

It might sound obvious but when there's a lot going on in life and routines might be askew, it can be all too easy to neglect basics, which can seriously affect our mood. Avoiding being hungry or tired won't make a bad situation magically better but not doing so can certainly make it feel worse.

So, keep a close eye on your child's diet and sleep to make sure they're in the best shape to deal with whatever is happening in their life. As they get older, teach them to do this for themselves and why it's important.

Smile (and the world smiles with you...)

There's a phenomenon called "emotional contagion" – basically, our feelings can go viral. Our kids can absolutely pick up on others' negativity, particularly parents' if they're looking to you to work out the appropriate response to a situation they haven't encountered before.

Nobody's suggesting you go around singing and dancing, or grinning inanely if something difficult is going on, but if it can be authentic and is appropriate, then encouraging a positive, happy vibe in your family can truly lift moods. Sometimes even just smiling can have quite a magical effect on ourselves and others – remember that line, "Smile and the whole world smiles with you"? It's at least a little bit true.

Get arty

Grabbing the crayons, colouring pencils or paints for some drawing, doodling or colouring in can be gloriously relaxing and mindful. In fact, creating art isn't just distracting and fun, it's known to reduce levels of the stress hormone cortisol and art therapy is a recognized approach to alleviating depression and anxiety.

If your child isn't exactly a budding da Vinci, it truly doesn't matter – this is more about becoming engrossed in the process, not the artistic merits of the end result, so be careful not to focus on what they produce as much as on the "doing" in itself.

Short on inspiration when faced with blank paper? Painting by numbers, colouring-in books, fuzzy felt or sticky mosaics kits are all winners for those who prefer a bit of guidance and structure for their arty, crafty ways.

Gather the good

Reflecting back on the day and working out what went well is an antidote to that negativity bias we talked about in Chapter 1. Here are a few prompts to help your child do this:

Today's top three

Whether it's over dinner or at bedtime, encouraging your child to highlight the three best things that happened that day can lead them to appreciate the positives in life and help them spot the sunlight even during difficult, darker times. It could be something as small as kindness someone showed to them when they were upset, a moment's laughter, a beautiful sunset, or an encounter with a sweet little dog or cat.

Rose and thorn of the day

One friend of mine has a variation on having a top three: at their evening meal, the whole family gives a "rose and a thorn" of the day – the rose being the best thing and the thorn being the worst. It triggers conversations about events and feelings and allows a balanced view.

Gratitude journaling

Keeping a gratitude journal won't just boost positivity at the time you write it, it can also form a lovely record of the things we have cherished in our lives. You can buy dedicated gratitude journals for kids or adults, but of course you could create your own with any notebook, which your child might like to decorate themselves.

Start some affirmations

We each have an inner voice and we can give it a prod, guiding it toward being more inspiring and positive and less critical and negative by programming in some affirmations.

An affirmation is a motto or phrase that we can get our inner voice to say whenever we need a boost or as a matter of routine on a daily basis – such as when we wake up in the morning.

Examples of some regular affirmations your child could try include:

- "I can do this"

- "I am not alone"

- "I am strong"

- "I am loved"

What could your child choose for theirs?

Imagine a happier ending (or beginning or middle...)

When that naughty negativity bias is up to no good again, making us imagine the worst outcomes and everything that can go wrong, it can be effective to reprogramme our thoughts by visualizing how things might go right instead.

Is your child imagining they'll start at their new school and have no friends... ever? Could they visualize a really happy first day?

If they are worried that Christmas will be awful now their parents are separated, could they think of a morning having fun with you *and* a lovely festive afternoon with their other parent too?

Just considering that such a thing is possible in their imagination can open the door to more positive perspectives. One option here is for your child to write a short story or description of how things might be and feel in a week / month / three months from now. Crucially, they have to give themselves a happy ending in their story.

Make a happy playlist

It's not just a hunch that cranking up the volume on a cheery tune has the power to lift our moods – research suggests listening to upbeat music really can make us happier (Ferguson and Sheldon, *Journal of Positive Psychology*).

Why not create a digital playlist of your family's best happiness boosters and keep it at the ready to brighten up any gloomy, grumpy moments? Here are some favourite toe-tapping, cheery tunes to consider including:

- "Happy" by Pharrell Williams
- "When You're Smiling" by Louis Armstrong
- "All You Need Is Love" by The Beatles
- "Bring Me Sunshine" by Morecambe and Wise (watch the ridiculously silly video of the pair singing this on YouTube too)
- "I'll Be There For You" by The Rembrandts
- "Happy Together" by The Turtles
- "What a Wonderful World" by Louis Armstrong (a happy chap, it seems)
- "Lovely Day" by Bill Withers
- "Don't Worry, Be Happy" by Bobby McFerrin
- "Walking on Sunshine" by Katrina and the Waves
- "I Can See Clearly Now" by Hothouse Flowers

CHAPTER 6

Dealing with life's biggest changes

While many of the general tips in this book will apply broadly, a few major life changes which children commonly face warrant special attention and specific advice: bereavement, parental separation or divorce and the arrival of a new sibling.

These are undoubtedly some of the most difficult situations to guide a child through, particularly when you are likely also managing your own feelings as well as dealing with practical matters at the same time. Given that, do make sure you have a read of Chapter 7 to find ways to look after yourself better too.

We also cover moving school and home here, as both can be very significant events for children to navigate.

Bereavement

The "when" – break the news as soon as sensibly possible

Sharing news of a loved one's death with your child can be daunting and difficult as you'll know it'll be heartbreaking for them and you will probably be very upset yourself. But it's important that you don't delay for too long, otherwise they might hear about it from someone else or overhear a conversation.

By letting your child know about the bereavement yourself, you can have a little more control over what is said, where and when (within reason). You can choose an appropriate moment and you can be there to offer hugs and reassurance, and answer any questions.

The "where" – choose your place mindfully

Find somewhere quiet and private to share what has happened. A place where your child can feel safe and secure if they cry or need a comforting cuddle without other people looking over and wondering what's going on, inadvertently making insensitive comments or asking questions your child is not ready for.

For example, if you collect your child from school and the death has happened during the day, it would be better to avoid telling them in the playground with their friends around or in the car all seat-belted up and unable to have a hug. Even if it is a struggle to keep things to yourself until you can be somewhere appropriate, it's probably best to wait until you get home and can sit down together and break the news to them.

The "what"

When it comes to what to say there's no set answer or specific wording, but a few general pieces of advice apply:

- Avoid euphemisms with younger children such as "Grandpa has passed on" or "Uncle John is no longer with us / has left us". These can be confusing (a young child might wonder where John has gone and why). The classic "X has gone to sleep now" can sometimes lead little ones to become afraid of falling asleep.

- Bereavement can lead to all sorts of questions from children – from the unexpected to the inappropriate. Deal with questions openly – if they're old enough to ask, they're old enough to deserve a reply. It's important to be factual and honest and it's absolutely fine to say you haven't got an answer to a question if you just don't know.

- Explain that it is okay to be upset and feel very sad. Be open about your own feelings – you don't have to hold your own emotions in to be a good, supportive parent; indeed, the opposite is true. If you end up crying together when you are sharing and then processing the distressing news with your child, that's absolutely natural and healthy.

- If needed, reassure your child that their loved one's death was not their fault or anyone else's (assuming that the deceased was not a victim of crime). Younger children can display "magical thinking" and might believe that they said or did something that caused or contributed to the death, or didn't do enough to prevent it happening, such as "I didn't stay at the hospital long enough and cuddle Grandpa enough, so he died".

Spend extra time together

Being there for and with each other in the aftermath of a bereavement is comforting and allows time together to remember the person who has died and reflect on what has happened.

As best as you can, try to spend some quality time with your child (and other close family) in the first few days, although of course if you were next of kin to the person who has died, you might well be busy trying to arrange the funeral and organize practical matters.

Talk with your son or daughter to see which of their activities and routines they want to continue in the first week or so after the bereavement and which they want to cancel. Do they feel comfortable going to school as usual or attending their after-school classes? Take their lead but have a backup plan and be sympathetic rather than cross if they change their mind at the last minute. It's also sensible to inform their teacher so that they can support your child and be attentive in case they get upset or behave differently to normal.

Keep an eye on your child's reactions – they can be unexpected

Children's reactions to bereavement can be very varied. Even the same child might respond differently at varying times – perhaps being fine at 7 p.m. while having their dinner but dissolving into tears just an hour or two later.

You might find your child reverting to behaviour from when they were younger – for example, a six-year-old who has been dry at night a while could resume bed-wetting, become fussier about food or stop sleeping reliably. On the other hand, they could surprise you by being especially mature beyond their years. Or it could even be a mix of the two. All this is totally normal.

That said, if your child's reaction is severe and persistent – beyond a few weeks of not being their usual self – and their well-being is not showing any signs of improvement, consider seeking outside support (see Chapter 8).

Be led by your child about the funeral

In previous generations, children were often kept away from funerals, but nowadays parents tend to take a more individual approach to the question of whether or not they should attend. There's certainly no hard and fast answer.

Some children find it comforting to be there: it helps them accept that their loved one has died. Others find the experience makes them even more upset – particularly if they will see the coffin. It really is a case of taking your child's lead.

It's sensible to have a contingency plan in case they change their mind at the last minute in either direction. Have a backup babysitter if they decide they'd rather stay at home after all.

If your child does go, find someone close they can sit with if you are involved in the ceremony, and who can take them outside if it all gets overwhelming.

If the person who died was very close to them and it would be appropriate, consider how your child can be part of proceedings, perhaps by choosing a piece of music or a reading, or contributing memories to the eulogy.

Mark their loved one's life in personal ways

Regardless of whether your child goes to the funeral or not, it can help them greatly to have their own separate, child-friendly way to mark their relationship and say farewell to the friend or family member concerned.

What might comfort and appeal will vary but ideas include writing a letter or poem, creating a memory book or box with photos and keepsakes, drawing pictures, visiting a special place they used to go together, or planting a tree with you.

These things can be especially useful if you're a family which doesn't have religious or cultural rituals to follow.

Divorce and separation

Whether your child knows you've been having relationship issues for some time or it will be a complete shock, separation and divorce – with all its finality and practical consequences – is deeply upsetting and unsettling for many children.

That said, your child ending up a distraught, damaged mess is far, far from inevitable – despite the narrative in everything from films to novels and from what friends and family might fear.

Some children really do take this situation in their stride, especially where there ends up being less conflict at home post-divorce compared to before, and where parents manage to maintain a relatively healthy co-parenting relationship for the long-term.

What's more, how you handle the aspects of your divorce and your family's life afterwards can make a difference to the outcome for your child – right from breaking the news through to the introduction of any new partners.

Tell your child together and plan what you'll say

If – and it really is a big if – you and their other parent are on amicable enough terms, the ideal would be to share the news together, allowing you to demonstrate that you're starting as you mean to go on and are still both their parents. Plan what you will say beforehand if you can be civil enough to do so, to avoid contradicting each other.

No matter how tempting it is to brush over things, it's better to be (fairly) truthful – as ever, in an age-appropriate way – about why you are separating. Otherwise your child will likely discover any misinformation later on, and they might feel their trust has been betrayed or it could confuse them.

An example of what you might say to a younger child is: "Daddy / Mummy and I are arguing and cannot live as nicely as we would like to any more. We still love you and are still both your parents but we need to live in separate houses. We will both see you [assuming this is the case] and have fun together and look after you."

For older children, go with an accurate explanation with as little blame as possible – another reason honesty is important with this age group is because they'll probably have seen and heard clues as to what's been going wrong with your relationship already.

Avoid "TMI"

Yes, be reasonably truthful, but do ensure your explanation doesn't slip into "too much information" territory, particularly around very personal aspects of your relationship (specifically sex, as frankly children always find it embarrassing and awkward to hear about that aspect of their parents' lives). Be as kind as possible about the other parent (absolutely not always easy, we know...) and try to avoid blame. They are still your child's mother or father and it's never wise to "bad-mouth" them to your child. If they have done something objectively awful, you can say you are upset with them about it, but try to remain as neutral as possible in front of your child.

More tips on talking about your separation

- Be clear that the separation is not their fault – younger children may believe that if only they had behaved differently, this might not be happening.

- Don't give them hope that you and their other parent might reconcile, if this is not a possibility.

- Explain that you and your now ex-partner still both love them and will do your best for them even if living arrangements change.

- Don't make them take sides or ask them to take a view of what's happened between you and your ex – it's not fair to do so (this is important for the long-term too). Feeling "stuck in the middle" of the conflict between you can make a child feel anxious, unsettled and guilty if they think they've been disloyal to one parent.

- This won't be your only opportunity to discuss all this with your child. The initial conversation will be the start of many; let your child know that they can come to you any time to talk about it further.

Prepare responses to likely questions

Try to anticipate your child's questions. It's impossible to think up all of these but the most common ones are:

- Why are you separating?

- Do you still love Mummy / Daddy?

- Whose fault was it?

- Where will we live?

- Who will I live with?

- How much will I see you both?

- Will I still get to see Grandma and Grandpa / my uncle / cousins (on your ex's side of the family) etc.?

- Will we have less money?

- Are you going to get married again and then have a baby?

- Can I still do X activity?

... but be honest if you don't know the answers yet.

Plan practicalities

Your child will almost certainly be worried about how their everyday life will be after the separation. Aspects of this you might want to consider as early on as possible include:

- The proportion of time your child will spend with each parent and how that will be split across the week / fortnight (obviously, sometimes this is subject to negotiations and legal decisions)

- Living arrangements – where will you live post-split and will your child have a bedroom at both homes?

- Arrangements for holidays, birthdays and Christmas or other key events

- Where any pets will be

- What will happen to their toys (younger children) or other key possessions
- Whether they will still see extended family members

In the early stages of separation, you might not know how all these practical arrangements will work out. If your child asks questions and you don't have an answer, it's fine to say you simply don't know yet, while reassuring them you will all be all right even if things are uncertain right now. Promise to update them when plans become clearer and try to keep that promise.

Looking to the long-term

Once the dust settles on initial arrangements, you've probably still got many years of co-parenting ahead of you. Here's some guidance about how to deal with the relationship with your ex for the longer-term good of your child:

- Don't "bad-mouth" your ex to your child, but be authentic about their other parent, especially with teenagers. If they are constantly letting your child down and not turning up for arrangements, for example, then it will seem phoney to your son or daughter if you deny what's going on and talk about their mum or dad blindingly positively. Respond to what they are saying about them and empathize but don't stoke it up further.

- Encourage your child to maintain a good relationship with the other parent – it's in your child's best interests to see both parents.

- Never use your child as a way to get back at your ex, for example by stopping them spending time together.

- Try not to compete with your ex for your child's affection or to be more popular – stick with strong boundaries and don't be tempted to spoil them out of guilt or competition. This is doing your child no favours in the long-term.

- If you are on reasonable terms with your ex, try to agree parenting approaches and rules that you are both satisfied with, as consistency will help your child feel secure. This is obviously tricky and can become contentious.

- The ideal aim is mutual respect rather than a blame game, but this can of course be challenging if you and your ex don't see eye to eye.

Introduce new partners cautiously

So you've met a new partner and you want them to get to know the most important person in your life: your child.

Some principles to bear in mind:

- Don't rush into the first meeting. There are no hard and fast rules on how long you should date before getting everyone together but stability is valuable for children, so wait until you're fairly confident that the new boyfriend or girlfriend is going to be around for the relative long-term. Being introduced to Mum or Dad's new partner, only to have you and them break up the following week, is not the sort of stability children need.

- After that, still don't rush it, even if your child seems to like your partner.

- Your child might take a little time to get used to your new partner and understandably might not feel as excited or positive about your relationship as you do. They might struggle to see many, or indeed any, upsides to it for themselves so don't be cross if they lack enthusiasm.

- It's usually best to introduce the new partner first and only later their children (if they have any), rather than all at once.

- It's nearly always best to meet "out" on neutral territory initially, so that your child doesn't feel your new partner is encroaching on their home space and routines. Basing this first meeting around a fun activity – such as bowling – that can be enjoyed by all ages can keep things relaxed.

A new sibling

Whether your child has been an "only" until now or already has one or more siblings, and no matter whether they're still a small child or a strapping teen, the arrival of a new baby to the family is a pretty seismic event.

It's safe to say that you can't always rely on your older child to be as delighted about your new addition as you are. They might feel any mix of emotions from excited to devastated or fearful, possibly swinging between all of these.

If they do have negative thoughts and worries or say things like, "I hate the baby," it's more constructive to accept the reality of this, rather than getting cross or telling them they should be excited and how wonderful it is to have a brother or sister. You'll make things easier all round by instead discussing their fears and then looking to address these together and providing reassurance (you might need to help them via the talking and listening tips in Chapter 3).

Focus on the short-term – sharing the long-term benefits of their new sibling is unlikely to have much sway. Right now, they'll be more concerned about being disturbed by a crying baby, a younger sibling using their toys or trashing their stuff and, most of all, having to share their loved ones – you and their grandparents.

Practical ideas for before the birth

Chat to your child about the prospect of their new sibling to help them feel involved. You could share information about the baby's growth, show them the scan photos and ask their opinion of your ideas for names, or get them to help choose things for the nursery, clothing or a gift for the baby. You might also want to suggest skills your older child might be able to teach their younger sibling or impress them with, such as Lego-building, drawing or entertaining them with a musical instrument. But be led by your child on this – if they aren't keen, don't force them or get annoyed if they don't want to play their part.

If your child isn't used to being around small babies, help them understand the realities of life with a newborn to give them an idea of what to expect. Explain that you might be tired and that the baby will mainly eat and sleep initially, so that these things don't come as a shock or disappointment. Also, share arrangements for their care before and immediately after the birth – ideally, have a family friend or relative come and look after them in their own home, rather than shipping your child off elsewhere.

Create a baby-free space – your older child might want to escape from the whirlwind of chaos that babies and toddlers can bring, and that should be respected. If at all possible, keep a room (usually their own bedroom) baby-free as their haven if they've had enough of nappies and noise and want to play without smaller hands coming and grabbing their stuff.

Practical ideas for after the birth

Retain some one-on-one time together – it's quite a challenge to achieve this when dealing with a newborn, but do your best to have time alone, just you and your older child. It could be as simple as you reading their bedtime story while your partner looks after the little one, or something longer such as going to the park or a café at the weekend, just the two of you. It's especially important to carve out some time together soon after the birth so your older child doesn't feel pushed out.

Many children feel understandably jealous when hordes of friends and relatives turn up at your home proffering gifts and attention galore to the newborn, while they look on ignored and empty-handed! Ask visitors you're close to if they can chat with your older child too – you could also ask them to bring a little something for them, or wrap a few goodies up for guests to give them. Older children might be cynical about this but a treat or gift "from the new baby" can go down well with younger ones.

And finally... be patient and make sure your child feels totally loved and secure with you, and the new baby hasn't changed that. Nobody can predict how close your children will be in the future, but chances are that over time your older child will bond with their brother or sister more. In the meantime, don't worry that you're doing something wrong and try not to get annoyed with your older child who is simply dealing with a huge change to their life in a very normal way.

Introducing older children to the family

Additions to the family are not always babies – they could be an adopted or fostered child or your new partner's child. This situation can be just as hard – and sometimes even harder – than a newborn's arrival. Respect your child's feelings if they aren't too keen initially but, at the same time, make it clear that you have firm boundaries about acceptable behaviour. Not being hugely enthusiastic and welcoming is okay (although of course not ideal), but being rude to or hurting the other child is not.

Encourage your child to get involved in appropriate decisions before the new family member arrives, if possible – could they help choose some toys or a "welcome basket" in advance? Again, if possible, have the first meeting out somewhere with an activity that they can bond over. In case conversation doesn't flow, have some "icebreaker" questions up your sleeve, such as favourite bands, foods, films or animals.

Moving school

School is a huge part of any child's life and changing schools is a major milestone. Their reaction to the move can depend on a range of factors, such as:

- How happy and settled they were at their old school

- Their personality – how confident they are socially and about change generally

- Whether they have moved schools before and how they found that

- How familiar they are with the new school / any pupils there

- Whether they are joining the school at the same time as other new pupils

- Whether they perceive there to be any upsides of the new school versus their old one

Overall, they might be excited or apprehensive, or any mix of the two at the same time! Use our talking and listening tips in Chapter 3 to gauge their feelings – discuss their impressions of their new school, what they might miss about their old one and what they're worried about. Then you can begin to gently address their concerns and use the ideas on the following pages.

Celebrate what they're leaving behind

Before focusing on the future, it's worth considering that many children will feel a loss about leaving their old school. This will usually be lessened if they leave at the same time as other pupils and if there are organized events such as a special assembly or leavers' party.

If, however, your child has moved on at a non-standard stage, especially mid-year, consider how you could mark their time at their old school. Here are some ideas:

- Create a memory book with pictures and memories about special moments and people.

- Have a café trip for a hot chocolate and cake, or a celebratory dinner at home, where you can discuss all their highlights and recollections of their time at the school.

- Write a letter of thanks with some of their memories to send to their teacher and class to say goodbye.

Be reassured that children often adapt to a new school relatively quickly and can soon move on from missing their old one.

Build familiarity with the new school

The more your child knows about the school they're off to and what to expect, the better – often it's the unknown that causes stress. To help:

- Attend any open days or taster sessions offered.

- Look around the school's online presence together. Some schools have video tours on their websites, which can be especially useful if you haven't managed a visit in person. You could also view a satellite map or street view of the school buildings.

- For primary or elementary school children, the class teacher is a particularly important figure. Request an introductory meeting with the class teacher and head teacher, or if they can't meet face to face, at least show your child a photo of them if it's on the school website.

- See if you can go to any events at the school, such as a summer fair, or a play, concert or sports event.

- If you know other children at the new school, can you arrange a meet-up so they'll have a familiar face when they start?

- Simply passing by the school can be helpful too. Point out any appealing or interesting features – that fun-looking playground equipment, or which classroom is theirs...

As the first day gets closer...

- Share any relevant information about the "day one" arrangements with your child.

- Find out what the school does to help new pupils settle in, especially if your child is moving outside of a normal starting point. Is there a buddy system, for example?

- Check for any concerns and questions they might have – little ones might be worried about what to do if they need the toilet, where they will eat and whether they will like the food, and how they'll find you at picking-up time. Older children and teens could be worrying about getting the uniform right and not being too "uncool", coping with more homework, fitting in or having to sit alone at lunchtime if they don't know anyone. For all ages, making new friends is a common concern.

- Be as prepared as possible for the first morning. Keep things more relaxed by ensuring that you know the route, that you leave enough time for the journey if there will be school-run traffic and, if you're driving, that you know where to park. Check which entrance your child needs to use too if there is more than one. If your child is older and will be travelling on their own, they could do a test run of the journey a few days beforehand.

- Ensure you have all the uniform and kit required and involve your child in choosing and buying this – a fun shopping trip might leave them feeling more excited and less apprehensive. A new school bag, stationery set or pencil case can make some kids feel more positive. Get everything ready the day before rather than in a rush on the first morning to make their transition as smooth and stress-free as possible.

On day one...

- Leave plenty of time to get ready, breakfasted and to school. When it comes to dropping them off, even if you're nervous yourself, try to remain relaxed and reassuring to your child. Offload to a friend, take a moment alone and breathe deeply, and put your best brave face on if you have to.

- With little ones, provide a quick reassuring kiss or hug but then encourage them on their way cheerily and positively. The staff will often be on hand to escort younger pupils in or you might be able to see them into the classroom yourself.

- Respect the wishes of secondary school-age children if they ask you to drop them off a little further away and prefer that you don't kiss or hug them (or make any fuss at all... or even talk to them!). This is their new world and it's understandable that they want to keep you at arm's length. Don't take it personally if they seem embarrassed by you!

> If your child is still struggling to settle in after a week or two, catch up with their teacher about how it's going and discuss any strategies that might help. Teachers are generally happy to talk over this kind of information and will want to work with you to support your child.

Moving home

Moving house is an upheaval for the whole family but can be especially unsettling for children, particularly if they've only ever lived in one home. They might well focus on what they're losing from leaving their old home rather than what they will gain at the new one.

Younger children might worry about whether their toys and teddies will get lost during the move, or about whether they will manage to sleep in their new room.

To help ease the transition:

- Involve your child in plans for the move or new home in appropriate ways for their age, so that they feel part of it rather than it being something happening "to" them.

- If possible, take them to visit the new house at least once after you've agreed your rental or purchase (so that the move is more certain), pointing out the positives as you go.

- Give them a say over relevant and appropriate things – choosing furniture for their new bedroom, how it is decorated, or where their favourite, familiar items might go.

- Try to get older children involved with a couple of suitable tasks before and on moving day, such as making lists or marking up boxes.

- Pack a dedicated "first night" bag together with their most treasured and important items, such as their teddy bear and usual nightwear, so you can keep an extra-close eye on it and make sure it's accessible for the first evening, rather than lost in a mountain of moving boxes.

- Create some continuity between a younger child's old and new bedrooms – their familiar bedding, alarm clock and bedside lamp can help little ones settle better for the first few nights.

- If you've moved away from your old area, help your child keep in touch with their friends there, ideally planning a reunion visit before long, if that's feasible, and if not, via a video call.

- Don't forget amid all the packing and organizing to check in with your child in the run-up to the move to see how they're feeling, so that you can address any concerns.

CHAPTER 7

Looking after you so you can look after your child

When focusing on guiding our children through challenging changes and putting their needs first, we can often end up neglecting our own well-being. It's not remotely selfish to look after yourself – and not just during difficult times either! In fact, by doing so, unquestionably you'll be better placed to care for your child, especially if you're dealing with the impact of the same event as them. A neat analogy is how adults are advised to put on their own oxygen mask before assisting children in the event of an emergency on a flight. It's absolutely in your child's best interests for you to devote some time to self-care so you're in a good place to parent. If you're struggling for whatever reason, here are some ways to help you through tough times.

Overcoming overwhelm

If everything's getting on top of you, leading to feelings of not being able to cope, here are some tactics to try:

- Manage one day at a time. If even everyday tasks seem like too much, shift from thinking too far ahead or seeking to fix everything now to focusing on taking on today for now. Just as for your kids, it's a case of "bird by bird" (see page 54).

- You only have to get through today, and then another day will start. You'll get through that, repeat and, chances are, things will feel a little differently before long. And remember that mantra, "This too shall pass" (see page 53).

- If you're overwhelmed with worry or panic, once you are sufficiently calm, ask yourself "What exactly am I worried about here?" and write a list. Then assess how big an issue each item really is, how likely it is to happen and what you might be able to do to ease it – similar to the exercise on page 63.

- If you simply have too much to do, focus on prioritizing your list and accept that you can only do your best in the time available.

Stay connected

When feeling wretched, the temptation to stay at home and hide away, tucked up under the covers or snuggled with a blanket on the sofa, can be powerful. You might lack the energy to spend time with others, or you might be too upset to face anyone and the potential for tactless comments or sympathy you can't cope with.

But, especially in the first few days of the aftermath of a difficult change, if possible, try not to shut yourself away at home – virtually or physically. Sometimes, if you can, it really is better to force yourself "out there" – to meet friends or experience something you normally enjoy which could be a ray of light, even if it doesn't appeal initially.

It could be as simple as going for a walk somewhere pretty or a coffee with one of your nearest and dearest who will proffer hugs and hankies when you cry. Start with familiar, more comfortable things that you know you can manage, and build up from there – but do make an effort to make little steps back toward your "normal".

If you find you want to stay away from your usual life for a sustained period, and the self-care tactics of the sort elsewhere in this book don't help, do look at the symptoms of depression we list on page 34 – they apply to adults as well as children. If you might be depressed, see Chapter 8 for advice on seeking external support.

Make space for some "me time"

It's a challenge with family and work commitments, but if you can, do prioritize taking a break – even just a few minutes each day – for yourself. It'll help you relax and leave space for you to think, reflect on and process the situation you're in.

It could be after the kids go to bed or before they wake up if need be – 10 minutes of quiet, journaling or meditation. Not looking likely? Can you pop the TV on for your child, and go and sit in an adjacent room, or in the same room with headphones and relaxing music on? Or get a neighbour or friend to babysit for an hour or two?

If other people's demands are meaning you don't have any time to yourself, consider whether sometimes you might be able to say "no" more for a while. If you're struggling, don't be afraid to put your needs first or turn down a social invitation if you'd rather do something quiet and restorative.

Focus on "good enough" parenting, not perfection

Modern parenting is unquestionably full on, with palpable pressure to provide a whirl of activities and outings, to manage our children's every moment and somehow create a perfect childhood, no matter what. Imagery of apparently perfect family lives on social media and in advertising doesn't help.

This is exhausting enough at the best of times but, right now, look at what non-essential activities and chores you can drop and don't feel guilty about it. That means not feeling guilty if the kids have another takeaway or ready-made meal for dinner, if you don't clean the house for a few extra days, if they watch a bit more television or if they are online more than you'd normally allow. It's really not going to do them any long-term harm and, if it helps you cope, then what's wrong with that?

Ensuring your kids are fed, clothed and safe, even if there aren't the usual modern parenting bells and whistles, is good enough – be kind to yourself about this.

Share but don't overshare with your children

On the one hand, it is unwise to try and conceal how challenging you're finding things from your children – they will work out something is wrong and it's better you explain it to them first-hand than they use their imaginations.

On the other hand, do avoid oversharing – if you need to offload, call upon a friend or grown-up relative or a professional.

To hit the middle ground, go with age-appropriate, child-friendly language to describe your own feelings and the situation, focusing on what your child actually needs to be aware of. "I'm struggling with this and I'm upset too but I know we will be okay and I'm getting help" is the right sort of tone.

Know you are not alone

You might feel that as a parent you have to be the strong one who looks after everybody else or, at times, that you're alone and nobody cares, but there's always support out there if you look for it. You really don't have to sit and struggle alone.

The most obvious option is calling upon your nearest and dearest for a shoulder to cry on or a spirit-lifting hug. You might feel like you don't want to trouble anyone else but any close friend or relative worth their salt will be there to support you as best they can – it really is what friends are for.

Beyond that inner circle, it can be hugely valuable to find others in a similar situation to yours, who will understand first-hand what you're going through and can share experiences. Search on the internet for relevant support groups or ask your doctor – there will inevitably be a website or a charity with information and advice, and often a free helpline.

Parenting forums have sections on bereavement, separation, and many other general parenting subjects. The charity Mind provides mental health information and advice.

For professional help, counsellors and psychotherapists can be extremely valuable, although unfortunately these services can sometimes be difficult to access through local or regional health services, and are expensive to pay for privately. If you're employed, check whether your company provides free or subsidized counselling services. Note too that some therapists work at reduced rates for clients who would otherwise not be able to afford their services.

Much of the advice in Chapter 8 applies to parents seeking professional support for themselves as well as for their child.

Seeking further support

As a society, we've seen a huge, welcome shift in attitudes about mental health and well-being. Where just a generation or two ago, there was all too often shame, embarrassment and lack of understanding ("Keep it to yourself", "What will people think?", "It's just her nerves"), now celebrities, sports stars, politicians and royals very openly discuss their own experiences and challenges. Alongside this, schools and employers make much more effort to promote education and openness about – and support pupils and staff with – mental health. Ways to get support are more visible and doing so is seen as being very normal and indeed a sign of strength rather than weakness.

If you do find yourself in a situation where your child needs further help, there's no shame, no stigma, no negativity to this. It does not make you a bad or failed parent and it does not mean there is something wrong with you, your child or your family. Quite the reverse: it shows you care and can recognize when your child needs support.

Where to look

Here are some of the most common sources of professional help for your child. There's no set answer as to which route you should go for and this will depend somewhat on the urgency of the issue and its type, waiting lists and affordability.

- If you are in the UK, make an appointment with your GP who might refer you on to the dedicated Child and Adolescent Mental Health Services (CAMHS). Unfortunately, at the time of writing these services can be quite hard to access, with lengthy waiting lists. Elsewhere, the equivalent would be your family doctor or paediatrician.

- Contact your child's school – some have a pastoral-care coordinator and even a dedicated counselling service. Like doctors, they can refer you to your area's mental health service. In the first instance, ask your child's class teacher or tutor if you are unsure of what might be available or who to get in touch with.

- Find a mental health professional directly, such as a psychotherapist, child psychologist, psychiatrist or counsellor (look via the relevant industry body for your country). For the rest of the chapter we call these "mental health helpers", shortened to MHHs.

- Call upon a charity related to the area of concern. For example, in the UK, there's Grief Encounter for bereavement, Gingerbread for children of separated or divorced parents, and Childline more generally. Some charities offer online support via their websites, as well as a more traditional phone helpline. These services tend to be better for short-term or ad hoc help before consulting one of the other options if needed.

- It can also be really useful to check out any specialist podcasts, books (written for parents or for children) or discussion forums that focus on the specific change situation your child is experiencing. The latter is a great way to get peer support from others going through the same or similar and to feel less alone.

When to seek outside help

Every child's situation and reaction to change is of course individual but, generally, it might be time to get outside help for your child if:

- They're showing signs of depression or anxiety (see pages 34 and 35).

- They're demonstrating behavioural difficulties that are hard for you or other family members to cope with and tactics of the sort that are in this book are not leading to any improvement.

- Their feelings or actions are getting in the way of them experiencing everyday life for a persistent period.

- They're self-harming or having suicidal thoughts, showing signs of eating disorders or hearing voices.

If you have serious, immediate concerns about your child's safety, obtain emergency medical advice.

Consulting a mental health helper – what you need to know

Whichever type of MHH you'll be speaking to, there are a few things that can help smooth the process and make it all the less daunting.

Before the first appointment

If your child doesn't yet know they'll be seeing an MHH, you could introduce the idea by starting a conversation about how they're feeling (deploy some of the tips in Chapter 3). Reassure them that the MHH will be there to listen and help them cope with what's been going on in their life but that of course they can always talk to you too.

If you haven't already done so, keep a diary (see page 49) – with your child, if they wish – for at least a week (the longer the better) beforehand to take with you, detailing moods, behaviours and any triggers.

You could also make and take some notes of any other relevant background information that will help the MHH get a clear picture of what's happening in your child's life and its impact on them and the wider family.

That said, the professional will be used to asking the right questions to assess your child's situation – it's very much their job to do so.

At the first appointment

Depending on your child's age, preference and the situation, you may or may not be joining them in the session. Check with the MHH and let your child know whether you'll be there or not. Usually, for under-16s a parent will be able to attend for at least part of the time.

It's natural for a child of any age to feel nervous, daunted or unsure about a first meeting with an MHH, but reassure them that there is no need to feel embarrassed or judged and that this is a "safe space" for them to express their true feelings. The professional will have heard it all before – they just want to help. This is important to remember for yourself too – they are not there to judge your parenting either.

The professional will ask you / your child about how they feel, how things are at home and school including any problems, their relationships and the situation. This first session might be more about understanding the issues and assessing whether their services are appropriate for your child at the moment. Be patient: advice or solutions will come in time in future sessions.

Confidentiality

Discussions with an MHH are a safe space for your child to express their feelings and share what is happening in their life. Whatever they say will be kept confidential from the wider world but it is sensible to have a discussion between you, your child and the MHH about what will be shared between you and what won't.

Inspiring quotes for tough times

For little ones…

> ## You are braver than you believe, stronger than you seem, and smarter than you think.
>
> Christopher Robin in *Winnie the Pooh*
> by A. A. Milne

For big ones...

> We delight in the beauty
> of the butterfly, but rarely
> admit the changes it has
> gone through to achieve
> that beauty.
>
> Maya Angelou

For you...

> # Learn from yesterday, live for today, hope for tomorrow.
> **Albert Einstein**

Conclusion

While we can't always change the situations life throws our way, we can change our reactions to them and how we respond. And that's very much what this book has been about.

Hopefully, it has helped you to help your child – not just with whatever they're experiencing in the here and now, but also with building strong foundations for their future to create a toolkit for tough times so that they'll be better equipped to deal with change resiliently and confidently throughout their life.

Because if there's one constant in the unpredictable world we inhabit, ironically, it's change itself.

About the author

Liat Hughes Joshi is a North London-based journalist and author who specializes in writing about parenting and family life. She is the author of six parenting books, published in 13 countries between them to date, and has contributed to many publications including *The Daily Telegraph*, *The Sunday Times* and *The Guardian*. She has been a columnist and agony aunt for Huffpost Parents and makes regular appearances on TV and radio providing comment on parenting, including on Sky News, LBC and BBC.

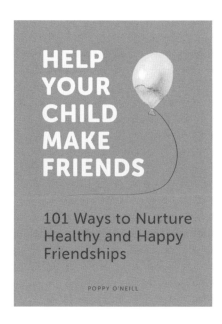

101 Ways to Nurture Healthy and Happy Friendships

POPPY O'NEILL

HELP YOUR CHILD MAKE FRIENDS

POPPY O'NEILL

ISBN: 978-1-78783-665-5

£9.99 UK, $13.99 US, $15.99 CAN

SEEING YOUR CHILD STRUGGLE TO MAKE FRIENDS IS DIFFICULT FOR ANYONE

Friendships can be tricky, but help is at hand. This guide will help you teach your child what makes a healthy friendship, and equip them with the tools they need to build stronger bonds and feel more confident in making new friends. Offering ideas, information and simple tips that will help you talk to your child and show them how to develop their social skills, this book will ensure they enjoy better friendships for life.

HELP YOUR CHILD DE-STRESS

VICKI VRINT

ISBN: 978-1-78783-673-0

£9.99 UK, $13.99 US, $15.99 CAN

72% OF CHILDREN SHOW BEHAVIOURS LINKED TO STRESS

Small amounts of stress are normal, but it can be difficult to know how best to support a child when they feel overwhelmed with worry. This practical guide offers strategies to help alleviate the physical symptoms and emotional signs of stress. By adopting simple tips, lifestyle changes and mood-boosting activities, you can help your child overcome challenging situations and live a happy and more carefree life.

101 TIPS TO HELP YOUR ANXIOUS CHILD

POPPY O'NEILL

ISBN: 978-1-78783-562-7

£9.99 UK, $13.99 US, $15.99 CAN

ONE IN FOUR CHILDREN WILL SUFFER FROM ANXIETY AT SOME POINT IN THEIR YOUNG LIVES

As a parent it can often be difficult to know how best to support your child when they become fearful and worried, and whether their worries are something they can deal with themselves or a symptom of something more serious. This guide offers ways to help you to help your child articulate how they are feeling and offers effective coping strategies and simple lifestyle tweaks to manage anxiety by building their resilience and self-confidence for life.

Have you enjoyed this book?

If so, why not write a review on your favourite website? If you're interested in finding out more about our books, find us on Facebook at **Summersdale Publishers** and follow us on Twitter at **@Summersdale** and Instagram **@summersdalebooks**.

Thanks very much for buying this Summersdale book.

www.summersdale.com